'We can only help others,
when we open up our heart'

— Angelica Ryder-Wood

The
Invisible
Thief

A collection of thoughts, reflections
and life's complexities

A Personal Anthology

by
Angelica Ryder-Wood

Book Bubble Press

Book Bubble Press
Published in the United Kingdom
First printed October 2019
Copyright © 2019 Angelica Ryder-Wood

A CIP record of this book is available from the British Library.

ISBN: 978-1-912494-51-4

Visit: www.bookbubblepress.com

DEDICATION

To my beautiful Mum,
I miss you dearly, every single day.

CONTENTS

The Hunter

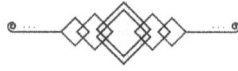

Readily searching, almost frantic,
for love.
Craving to be desired.
Outward appearances seduce
like shiny buttons to a pilfering magpie.
Not choosy
once chosen, they come, they go.

Desperate to fill the void
with anything, with anyone.
Not soul searching, superficial glances, lack depth.
Gauze over a wound that never heals.

At last, entrapped within
a love so powerful,
beautiful and raw.
Panic descends
with pain and self-destruction.

Rejected swiftly, with bluntness agog;
He retreats into the darkness
of another life, a painful reminder.

The pain steadily dissolves,
sorrow overwhelms.
The pattern jammed forever on repeat,
over and over.
New lover, old lover, new lover.

All treated the same way,
lavished with outlandish offerings.
Reaching goddess heights.
Wanting for nothing, except love.

Too close, too needy, yearning for more.
In flight mode.
The switch barely flicked,
then discarded,
like an unwanted gift.
Used.

Anger follows, then bitterness.
Feelings taut as a bowstring.
Once more hurting, pain gnawing.
Memories flash, his internal video screen
frozen with every blink of an eye.
Playback. On repeat. Out of control.

Desire to buy. Materialistic.
An adrenaline high.
A drug.
Temporarily numbing the hurt.

Excitement filters, pain and reward,
fixed for a fleeting moment.
Euphoria even. The high.
Short-lived.
Dependent, the needy fix.
The depths slump with roller coaster speed.

Boredom rears its devilish head,
the desire for a new challenge.
Emotions rise, control held tight.
Choking the memories before they surface.
A comfort blanket, smothering rationality.

Needing to hunt, watching behind no more.
The hunter, not the hunted,
but haunted with hurt.

Waiting for Him

Waiting for him,
to take me.
It comes to us all, sooner than you think.
Youth flashes by, at lightning pace, a blink.
Maturity is not a given,
it's a gift.

How much wasted time?
Regrets?
Wrong decisions or decisions never made?
Paths not followed. I wonder.
I wait.

If I had my time over
How different, how fulfilling...
Would love find me once more?
Would love leave me once more?
To fend for myself,
I wonder.

Would children I father?
Grandchildren too? Would I see them?
Those mountains I climbed, would they still be there
waiting?

Would I be bold? Confident and strong?
Yet compassionate and kind?
Would I fight for my country?
Bravery awarded. Proud.
I would.

Time moves quickly, faster each year,
it draws towards Him. Steadfast.
Am I wanted? Always.
Has my purpose been served?
Have I done all I could possibly do?
I have.

Thoughts scare. Am I prepared?
Endings are beginnings.
Another journey, one not travelled.
Will I welcome it, arms wide?
I will.

Father's Pride

Decisions, never easy.
Flip a coin? Take a chance?
Plan a strategy, the grown-up way, right?
Follow your heart? Or head? Or the latest idea?
Father wants you to be a doctor, not a dancer.
Mother wants grandchildren, two at least.
A boy and a girl.
Alex and Abbey, she says...

Choices are made, are they yours?
Teachers? Parents or peers?
Which one is right? Which one is wrong?
Follow money, says Father.
Follow love, says Mother.
Follow me, says her sporty boyfriend.
Follow me, says her academic sister.
Don't look back, grandpa says,
always wise, he of few words.
Grandma wants happiness, contentment and joy.

What do I want?
To make others happy?
Disappointment if I choose a selfish path.
Losers always lose.
Not everyone can be satisfied.
In pleasing one, others will feel rejected, unimportant.

'Dancing isn't a career, it's a hobby, a pastime'.
I'm sure they are right. Even for the talented.
I will grow out of it, they say.
If I get injured, then what?
No career.

A doctor it is. Decision made.
But a vacuum of emptiness.
Father's pride could not satisfy the apathy,
Nor share his excitement.
He sees a career, money, success.
I see parental bragging rights.
A status not desired.
I want him to be proud,
more than I want to follow my own selfish path.
It is selfish.

The Shadows Are Never Alone

Darkness falls,
frantic barking breaks the silence.
Staring into the inky night, fixated and wary,
he sees what mortals can't.
His senses acute, he backs into the corner, afraid.

The thuds,
the footfalls,
always rhythmic,
a bouncing ball... almost.
Loudly, then fading into the distance,
gradually.
It scares the youth.
They see ghostly forms,
petite, ethereal, drifting.
Fleetingly then gone.
A figment? A fragment?
No, adamant.

The voices scare, 'Psst, come here', they say,
almost inaudible.
In darkness, the eerie silence broken by whispers.
Gender unknown, but belief is absolute.
The balloon,
gliding purposefully along the passageway.
How?
Silver hairs drifting lazily down,
entwining into quizzical minds.

Feathers, white, soft, beautiful... floating gracefully.
The black one bears sombre news.

Unsettled,
they stay, they go, unable to endure the whispering.
The gentle blowing, the presence of whom?
Strapping adolescents, broad-shouldered,
fearful of... their imagination or something more?
Not sinister, surely?
A sense of humour not everyone shares.
You can almost hear the cries of laughter.

Calmness follows, protected almost,
swathed in a heavenly cloak...
Fingers gently stroking sleepy faces,
reaching out beyond universal reality.
Take notice. Hear them. Be guided.
Believe.
Beyond the darkness, a celestial presence,
always watching.
The shadows are never alone.

Shrunken

Towering above,
a perspective like no other.
Vascular, lanky limbs, out of control.
A gangly giraffe...
A beacon of awe, young and old, stare mercilessly.
Pointing,
heads turn... a freak show
nature created to amuse.

Awkwardness assumes, head bowed,
shoulders stooped,
covered in ill-fitting attire,
hanging loose like sackcloth.

No avoiding the questions, how many times today?
No escape for an introverted, insular soul.
Words mumbled; steps stumbled.
Collar turned high,
embarrassment higher.
Beard concealing, collar-length hair disguising... feral brows.
Almost hiding those sorrowful, earthen eyes.

His escapism, a virtual world beyond,
lost behind a lens of imagination.
The idyllic hideaway.
Creating images of what could have been.

Running from what he could never be,
yearning for what he could never have.

Never forgetting, blink and he sees,
vivid imagery.
Memories ingrained,
forever.
Pulse racing, bony hands clammy,
breath rapid and shallow.
A hint of a smile beneath copper, peppered whiskers,
as he remembers.
Fondly.

Reaching out, though never quite touching,
his strength in another.
Out of reach but never out of sight,
longing for the unconventional life,
she brings.

With freedom, joy, and love entwined.
To embrace acceptance within.
He bides his time, heart lifted.
For one day.
Soon.

Virtual Delusion

She dreams wistfully
of life beyond the moment.
Visions of betterment, body-hugging security.
Curiosity
of an existence never quite reached,
but desired so desperately.

Scrolling, she gazes, lost in a false world of pretence,
of extravagance,
of gaiety.
A smile never quite reaches their eyes.

Riches on show, like a garish window display,
a newborn for the world to admire.
Enticing the needy, the awe-inspired
wanting to belong.
Shallow, yet successful,
empty yet fullness brimming over.
If only behind the facade, reality shone through.

The lies,
not truth,
no different.
She has more, but less.
She dreams.

Feeling inadequate, they race ahead,
gathering momentum and followers aplenty.
Fanning their ego, words gushing,
sharp tongues quickly diminished into the delete pile.
Their filtered perfection and abundant possessions,
ostentatiously on show...
Narcissistic nobodies.
Behind the falseness, a vacuous emptiness,
of vulnerability and pain.

The need,
to be wanted. Desired. Admired.
Insecure yet brash,
opposites mindlessly battling their outcome.
Is this their reality?
Or a virtual illusion in a virtual delusion?
She dreams.
Of contentment.

Never Met You

Do you look like me?
Strawberry blonde, neither flaxen nor red,
or is that auburn like mother?
Irritatingly wavy, neither curly nor straight?
Bleached to erase the childhood taunts,
of my natural hues.

I will never know

Tawny eyes, my strongest feature
I'm often told,
twinkling mischievously.
Changing colour, chameleon-like
to reflect my moods and nature's seasons.
Freckles faded in winter,
a smattering, shyly surfacing with summer rays.

I will never know

Do you have monkey toes too?
Longer than fingers,
freakish even.
Can you dangle upside down
holding on with your digits,
grasping tightly until the blood drains away?

I will never know

Is a map of the world, etched into your palms?
A sign of an active mind they say,
better on your hands, than on your face, I laugh.

I will never know

Do we share the same humour?
Do you laugh out loud?
Spew gibberish tales to yourself?
Do you dance around the house with wanton abandon?
Are you carefree, independent and strong?

I will never know

Do you love all animals, even more so than humans?
Their quirks and loyalties hold no bounds.
Do you prefer being alone
sat with your thoughts,
reading an eclectic selection of genres?
Do you listen to music? What kind do you like?
Pop? Classical? Jazz or Soul?
Aretha or Michael?

I will never know

Would you travel the world?
Are you freedom loving, and just a tad eccentric?
Me too!
Do you love helping others?
Maybe volunteering in vibrant African villages?
Fighting for elephant conservation,
or teaching, willing, wide-eyed children to read?

I will never know

Would you rather spend your life as a cubicle dweller?
Working nine-to-five, retiring at sixty?
Comfortable pension,
and the much sought-after golden handshake.
I bet not!

I will never know

Do you prefer sunrises or sunsets?
Beaches or woodland? City or country?
Would you get married and have children?
Or spend your time seeking the meaning of life?
Are you religious?
Spiritual or agnostic?

I will never know

Do you drink wine?
Red, luscious and fruity.
Or white, sparkling like your eyes in the sunshine?
Perhaps beer from a bottle is more your style?
or sobriety even, like me?

I will never know

Are you vegetarian like father?
Or pescatarian like me?
Or maybe a carnivore, like our darling brother?

I will never know

We've never met,
we never will - in a physical embrace.
I was oblivious of your fleeting existence,
a chapter of my life never revealed.
Hidden away for decades.

You,
the dark secret everyone knew but me.
Never fear,
our kindred souls will cross paths in time to come,
and then

I will know.

Everything but Nothing

Outwardly proud, with grand possessions,
his lavish lifestyle.
Showing all, his status, prosperity, success.
Envied by many, hated by few.

Everything but nothing

Loved falsely, hidden intentions unknown.
He trusts cautiously, cheap words surface level.
Lacking meaning, lacking depth.
Lacking.
Inner strength empty, almost worthless.
Satisfaction bleak, emotions drained,
grieving for love never known.

Everything but nothing

Emotionless, shoulders slumped
an emptiness words cannot describe,
"How can one with so much be so unsatisfied?"
They mock.

"Easy"
Whispers the reply,

"When you have everything but nothing"

Save Our Souls

Obsessive thoughts, the persistent voices,
such relentless torment.
His fragmented world draping listlessly.
Carried upon burdened bones,
smothering every morsel of weary life,
like a fire blanket dampens angry flames.

From every direction,
overwhelm swamps.
Internal voices deafen any rationale.
Lacking clarity, hope, or escape.

His body wizened,
bleak emptiness lingers
with nefarious destruction,
bleeding from every orifice of a once robust mind.
Choices.
The dark ones, seep out,
mocking...

His lowest ebb, the inky darkness calling.
Whispering, it beckons.
Devilish features, gnarled.
Imaginary eyes glinting,
offering a promise of a resplendent future.

It lies. It taunts.
Luring vulnerable souls into a vortex of disillusional trickery.
If only the blind could see its selfish intentions,
blinkered into a state of tunnel vision hopelessness.
Draining every last remnant of life...

The end brings relief.
Yet devastation.

Save our Souls...

'Lord' of Delusions

Delusional? Ideas of grandeur and glory.
Fat Cubans, smoke drifting lazily,
through flared nostrils and beaded sweat.
His silken gown, oriental, taut.

The indulgence apparent,
laden with sovereignty, brash at best.
No title; *"Oh Lord,"* they smirk.
Chest swells, straining, new veneers gleam
brighter than his intelligence could ever be.

Oak-stained doors, weathered,
the past belies the truth.
Once-panelled walls, warping into shabby - no chic.
Status is life, past luxury that once was
now long gone.
Replaced with ageing artefacts,
tattered, broken and rusted.

Nicotine-stained fingers,
prosperity squeezed around each bloated digit.
The crest of an unknown quantity, fading
into nine carats of a poor investment.

The once resplendent English motor,
musty, unused.
The covers, laden with dust and disrespect.
Leather cracked, mirroring its owners
sun-beaten skin.

The Easy Life

His thinning hair,
auburn, silver, and mocha,
weaving through a lazy beard.
Waistline thickening, alcohol levels rising.
Pristine trainers. Expensive. Crude.

Black studded belt, khaki hipster combats
tattoo-covered chest, lacking symmetry or thought.
Skulls, roses, badly etched lettering,
adorning sunless skin.

The easy life, clocking in, clocking out,
occasional overtime.
Too many nights wasted in bars,
drunken stupors a given.
Lacking prospects, ambition or passion.
No goals, no dreams,
just the easy life.

He was besotted,
she was his everything,
his entire existence.
Bewitching him,
more than any wonderment of his expectant imagination.
His forever girl,
vivacious and alluring,
her spirit for life, contagious to all, but him.

She demanded more than he could provide,
love with passion.
Envisaging a future. The dream.
Her dream.
Not drifting aimlessly through life.
Love was not enough...
For her.

She drifted,
slowly away... making excuses, easing the pain.
Not wanting to hurt.
She moved on swiftly, another in her sights.
Devastation consumed his every waking moment
and every shadowy, sleepless night.

Whiskey, his medicinal crutch,
his heart eternally shattered.
Fragile. Weak. As he.
A void never quite healed.
A love never forgotten.
For him.

A Simple Man

For money not love
The path travelled
Feet drag, slowly
Trudging wearily
To a place not desired

Too late to change
No looking back
Blinkers leading
One foot steady
One foot follows

In too deep
Claustrophobic
Sweating
Wanting change
Secretly wishing
Wings could fly

High, soaring above
Looking down
With warmth
Freedom from restraints

A simple man
His pen, neat with ink
As black as tar
Paper, backed with love

A simple man
Trapped in existence
No pleasure,
Contentment fled
Like the fox
Chased by thirsty hounds

One day
When old, stooped
Thoughts dimmed
Far too late
For a simple man

Sacrificed for What?

The pungent aroma of death
lingers low in the mist.
The pounding of hooves on dirt,
disappears into distant pastures.

A blackbird sings for sorrow is nigh.
A rabbit scampers, another day of chance is over.
Blood-sodden fields tells the tale of life,
sacrificed for sport.

A mother mourns her lowly son,
a human's perspective is not considered this day.
The cries, blend into mayhem and lather.
Sweat clings, blood drips, deafened by noise.

Bloodshed and unknown fear carry on.
Hearts thumping wildly, bodies quivering,
anticipation for the outcome of life.
Slow motion is, thus, painful the hurt.

Eyes haunted with fright, the end drags on.
Jaws wide with hunger, eyes fixated,
possessed with an instinct to kill.
Innocence has no chance against beast,
but why is man the enemy as well?

Time's Gone

As a youth I had a plan
Hopes and dreams
Vivid pictures, crystal clear
The path led forward
That much I knew

Along came my twenties
And partying came too
Priorities changed
The path bent sharply
Dreams were blurred

Thirties came with crossroads
My twenties gone
The pressure now on
Career versus children
My path carried straight on

Forties flew by
With meetings and schedules
No time to think
No time to daydream
The path stayed straight

Fifties slowed down
Time to reflect
On the hopes and dreams
A distant memory
Of what could have been

The regrets set in
So deep, like furrows
The loneliness
Never sharing, never caring
No love, just emptiness

The path had been straight
But so hellishly fast
Dreams passed me by
With nothing to show
For my chosen path.

No End

Furrowed brow
Enthusiasm glows
Deep concentration
Lightning speed changes

Scattered mindlessly
Chaos surrounds
Madness follows
Entrenched in layers

Boredom beckons
Fighting the battle
Laughter, mocking
A wry smile
Anger prevails

Awakening passion
Heads turned
Focus dissipated
Squandered within

Echoes mocking
Frustration cries
Torment lies deep
No end no beginning

The Other Side

If I could talk to you,
what would I say?
Questions not asked,
secrets hidden.
What have you not told me?
What do I not understand?

The smiles, the caring,
an abundance of love.
What lies deeper
behind those eyes?

Buried away, secrets untold.
So many questions,
stories to unfold.
Why?

What drove a gentle spirit?
Was it fear?
So many questions,
not shared, entombed,
between us and the grave.

Whatever the past,
unconditional love,
will never die,
for you.

Divided Always

Not broken, nor bleeding
Shrivelled, foetal-like
Driven, she fought
Forward, seeking

No quitter, proud
Dry eyes bleak
Chilled through nights

Awakened the ghost
Haunted it teases
Never wanting,
Always mocking

Drenched in hatred
Love had never lived

Only shallow graves
Deadened by sins
His lies never began

Enemies within
Treading through fear
Empty vessels retreat

Hopeful for victory
Abashed, fallen

Death grows easy
Ending paths; forward
Peace flows graciously
Horizons bloom

Arms lay close
Entwined as one
In joyous love

Stronger feast,
Alone no battle
United with connection

Mountainous in victory
Walk, the path
Once walked before.

The Ambivalent Salesman

Can't quite fathom.
Why?
His superficial feelings, surface level.
No depth, structure or empathy.
Passion lacks passion,
it fizzles.
Slowly, then quickly.
Can't quite fathom.
Why?

Apathetic or just pathetic?
Indecisive, his life passes by.
Decades drag in a
drunken, smoked-filled haze.
Fast food
completes his fast life.
Worldly, yet lacking.
Depth. Insincerity. Transparency.
As a whole.
His silken lines, banter of old.
No substance, unsure,
of self.
Oh why?

Her realisation of inherent shallowness,
dawns, slowly.
Relief oozes, shoulders relax.

Set free, she embraces the savannah
Its intoxicating beauty.
Its expanse,
spread before her.
Run. Run fast.
No devotion, no tethers.

Sunlight entices, beckoning
with comely light,
So clear and cloudless,
illuminating her path.

Gone the depressing drudgery.
His bitterness, draining time from
her short life.
Oh why?

A Magicians Illusion

Fear,
strangles two-handed.
Smothering, with blanket dampening thoughts.
An illusion not tangible.
Breath crushed, gasping.
Carrying the grief.
whilst burdening all.

Fear,
nourishing the dread.
Ushered into the fold,
an old friend, maybe the enemy, or both?
Watchful, patiently waiting, opportune moments arise.
It welcomes and rears, in all its ugly splendour,
and charm.

Fear,
a rapid, advancing disease takes hold,
dredging the organs of sanity.
Manipulating the devoted,
weaving its spell on the unsuspecting.
Spreading through every existence.

Unveiled

Unveiled, she stood
Fully clothed, yet bare
Watchful eyes, with admiration and awe
Who made this beauty?
She reads their minds with ease

The applause slow, steadily rising
The roar, almost deafening, rapturous
The chants, the clapping
A thousand faces given the chance

To believe
In something more,
Almost cult-like in belief
Staring
In amazement
Both sides inspired

Not a word spoken, but collectively understood
The beauty
Inward, yet seeping out
Veiled no more

The Final Destination

Drowning in thoughts, ideas, imagery.
The noise humming steadily,
rising upward, deafening.
Visual overload, stimulating the senses beyond
all recognition.

Internal combustion verging on probability.
Anxiety awaits, confusion belies.
Is a lobotomy the answer?
Desperate to quash the voices,
respite only comes through darkness falling.

Where to start?
Distractions aplenty.
Flitting from one wordless action to another.
Lacking purpose or plans.
A desire to want and create so much.

Partially completed projects,
boredom, drifts with the latest idea...
Lacking focus, frustration mocks,
knowing the limits, not pushing further.

Never stretching enough,
just out of reach...

The Final Destination

The First Time

Dewy grass, laden
with twinkling dawn stars.
Scent crisp, uplifting
lungs gasp, inhaling.
The newness. Strange yet
familiar, comforting.

Turn the page. Neither
chapter nor verse laid
before me, waiting.
Enticing, excitable to begin,
expectations soar. Lifting higher,
anticipation nears.

Strain, morning breaks,
awkward silences,
unnerving palpitations.
Beaded brows. Newness.
Novel not accepted,
teasing, cat-like.

Murmurs and sniggers
over droopy heads.
Arrogance leers. Emptiness
guided by the pack. Misfits follow.
Vacant thoughts
retreat once challenged.

Wings beat, rapidly.
Its thunderous sound
alerts passers-by.
Chest swollen, as love
filters into
cavities unknown.

Delicate beings
cocooned. Comforted.
Nurtured.
Latched onto a familiar soul
bound eternally,
intertwined by kinship.

Whispers, through dishevelled hair.
Breasts rising,
her breath, barely audible,
rapid and shallow. Eyes wide.
Anticipating, wanting.
The unknown, ready to receive.
Waiting willingly.

Damaged

Scowling, he questions,
she frowns.
Heavy brows furrowed.
Bemused, almost quizzical, head tilted.
His eyes full of mistrust, burrow deep,
probing to find answers.
Finding nothing but denial and puzzlement.

Born into instability, beaten, abused.
Lesser than a beast,
hidden scars weeping.
Outwardly charming,
the chatter, a gent.
In the shadows, rage rears.
Spittle lingers
like a cruel spectator.

Shaking with bewilderment,
His fuse lit.
Fists taut, arms flailing
no direction, no cause.
Pain he gives to feel comfort – his
release.
She's blameless,
the innocence is unknown.

He walks away,
control with words,
control with actions,
lacking control.

She sighs, calm restored,
thoughts return.
Happiness sucked down,
a vortex of guilt
for no reason.
Her eyes close,
lids heavy.

Laden amongst the flowers
the warmth of the sun,
the gentle breeze.
She breathes slowly,
expanding each nostril.
Inhaling honeysuckle,
the sweet scent of innocent life.

Her retreat,
peace descends momentarily.
Relief and normality returns,
before doubt creeps in
weaving its cruel jibes once again.

The Depths

Bereft of love
Soaked in fear.
Always
blinkered,
Failed by society.

Void of emotion
Lacking, worthlessness.
Life carries on,
shining
in all its worldly splendour.

Blackness lingers
in hidden depths.
Asphyxiating positivity.
Tension coiled, spring-like.

Meaningless in reality,
despair rears violently.
Felling its victims.
drowning and pained.

Desensitised,
Solitary they roam.
Distanced from
civilisation.
Entwined into the core
of self-destruction.

The narrowing tunnel,
powerless, deafening.
It captures.

Helplessness falls into
desolation.
Imprisoned within,
nobody hears.

Inadequacy triumphs,
the cries unheard.
Failure looms expectantly.
Its victims, its victory.

Happiness... The Illusive Wanderer?

It's intangible, immeasurable
escaped by many, desired by all.
Manifested through universal thoughts.
Indulgences contribute to short-term fixes.
Highs, lows... smiles, tears of laughter,
washed away with salty sadness.

Materialistic tendencies,
always grasping, always wanting,
trying to capture the impossible.
Clinging desperately to feelings of euphoria,
of enlightenment, of peace.
Visions of perfection,
jumbled with reality.

Rose-tinted, judgement clouds
shifting desires to another level
of happiness.
The deserved gain, what the undeserved crave.

Who chooses?
Do we all experience that illusive, transient emotion?
It appears, albeit fleetingly,
then vanishes, shared amongst many,
the wanderer it travels.

Reaching out to the masses, yet passing most by.
Happiness...
Not taken for granted nor expected,
only the deserving,
encounter the soul-given warmth.
The chosen few,
embrace the momentary beauty
and savour the often unimaginable...

Purgatory

Floating in neither existence,
an abyss.
Limbo, a place of lack and confusion.
The unknown but not alone,
decisions removed, above or below?

Time has no place, a standstill.
Waiting—patiently.
Who decides our souls' outcome?
A time to reflect on life's lessons,
the ebbs and flows.
The scales of balance embrace power.

Do the bad decisions outweigh the good?
Is the higher being, hawk-like?
With one giant eye or billions, watching?
Filming life, recording every movement.
Waiting to be shown our final destination.

Do we all reside in purgatory?

Flying Higher

Soaring above, oblivious to worldly distractions.
Cocooned, protected, overwhelmed with freedom.
Wings beat, faster, momentarily pausing to
scan the horizon.

Clouds of hope,
billowing mattresses of warmth.
Welcoming, a long-lost soul reunited.
Carefree,
disappearing into the ether
here one breath,
vanishing with another.

Silently they sweep,
hovering.
Wings beating,
a gentle breeze wafting through shades of azure,
turquoise and milky opaqueness.

Shoulders lifted,
weights feather-like
lightness and joy,
shimmering in newness.
Once lowly,
hopelessly enslaved knowing nothing but drudgery.
Misery the norm.

Bound no more, unleashed ... dreaming high,
flying higher...

Impatience of Youth

Distractions,
a jumble of ideas tumbling around my head.
Filtering thoughts
Good? Bad? Possibilities?
Where to start?
Which to follow?
Which to ignore?

Who knows the path of success?
Studying faded,
worldly path more fruitful.
Impatient for rewards... desire for admiration.
Serving time, working hard,
rewards few, craving victory.

Instant gratification,
no effort, easy not lazy.
Drawn to him, not chasing the dream.
With highs and lows,
pressure strengthens, eyes watching,
waiting for the mighty to fall.
Mistakes are plentiful.

Goaded by peers,
jeered when success shows its bleak cloak.
Emotions dive,
lower than the damp earth.
Watered by frustration not perspiration.

Mood deepens,
unwavering in its misery
another day beckons.
Hope rises with amber skies
expectations high...
But does the dawn of reality rise too?

Who am I?

Who am I?
Unemotional, blank
Smothered, dictatorial
Who is she?
Unrecognisable, unsmiling
Lacking no compassion,
Cold to the core
An empty vessel
Of what once was
Gone now, long gone
Devoid of life,
Spirit, hope, and happiness

Bleak future
She died inside
Spirit broken
Stolen unbeknownst
Flailing into the depths
Weak with fighting
Her body lies limp
Lifeless

Her mind, brainwashed
Restricted thoughts
Bound and controlled
Beyond recognisable
By her, by them
Who is she?
Who am I?

The Captured Heart

Gently thawing, it flutters,
wings slowly spreading, gaining strength.
Breaths of air gulping the purity,
from darkness the glimpse of light,
silently peers.

Unlocked from its shackles
no longer bound by loneliness.
Warmth seeps in,
flowing through a venous maze.

The heat envelops a cloak of hope
soaring upwards, beating rapidly.
A butterfly no longer cocooned by despair.
The light beckons, brandishing rays, streaming golden glints.

The clouds part,
indigo skies outstretching,
Wanting.
Embracing the newness.
The longing dissipates,
rebirth breathes life, drenching every cell.

Treadmill

Eyes wide, sky black, in starless silence
thoughts pour, no relief,
enjoy the silence.
Running late, heart rate climbs...
pounding wildly, ready to explode.

Metal boxes protecting,
travelling to a predestination.
Scenery passes by, as life does too.
The thoughts plague never evaporating.
Longing for stillness, contentment.

Outwardly calm, inner sanctum turbulent
teetering on the verge.
Can't stop, guilty at rest.
An agitated mind, constant self-persecution.

Juggling responsibilities, craving a twin soul
darkness closes, eyes weighty,
dreams torment.
No escape, the treadmill unabating
continuously erratic, invading the stillness.

The Cult

Sweat pools, between heaving breasts,
voluptuous and glistening.
Heart flickering,
faster, more erratic.
Beads drip,
the saltiness a comfort.
Tasted.

Pounding,
a band of drums, louder.
No room for escape,
no respite.
Lights glaring, unbearable,
through the opaqueness no solace.

Stabbing,
in perfect harmony with the drums,
between bruised eyes.
Slight movement, excruciating.
Once-taut muscles, limp and lifeless,
beyond feeble.
Pathetic, laden and heavy....
Pain burrows,
deep into the soul,
no space left untouched.
Its presence felt in every screaming orifice.

Mind and body poisoned; the fight lost.
Battled with honour,
victory waned.
Bed-ridden and exhausted,
dignity shattered,
weakness the failing.
Its territory claimed, wounds carried forever.

Lady of the Night

She stands alone,
deserted by all,
distanced from her family.
Waif-like and gaunt,
cheekbones protrude.
Her skirt so short,
to tempt and to tease.

Tenderness and innocence sold to a stranger,
emptiness dwells in her soul.
Night after night she waits
hating them,
but hating herself more.

Her body a public possession, not her own
used, abused, discarded.
Only a kiss sacred.
She injects to forget
her memory hazy,
her body lies numb.
The anaesthetic soothes.

Their faces vivid,
sick and disturbed.
Haunting.
She waits for hours in wind, and snow.
The vicious circle on nightly repeat.
She's somebody's daughter
bruised and scarred.
danger lurks ever near.

Sacrificing life, day after day,
morning dawns once more.
A deal is struck, her purse empty.
The hit brings relief, temporarily.
It deadens her sadness and aching limbs.

True Intentions

The guises mixed,
his unknown intentions
lie beneath the charade.
Expectations shattered,
splintered into emotional shards
they tear deeply.

A masterful wordsmith,
Meaningless, with shallow dreams.
Once broken, abandoned,
dredged through a fog of confusion.
Clarity faded, beaten and bloodied
left in uncertainty.

To wonder,
the meaning, the outcome.
His staunch beliefs deep-rooted, unchanged.
Helpless, unless perfection is sought.
His unachievable boundaries laid bare.

Mocking... jeering... daring to challenge
His eyes wide, his vulnerability oozing.
Wounded hearts scattered.
Apologetic, darkness rises, thoughts drift.

A broken soul,
listless, stooped over,
defeated and powerless... morphing into one again.

Misunderstood

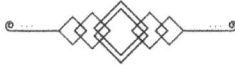

Demonised for her mistaken words,
confused, lacking.
In bewilderment she stands,
wide-eyed, mouth tense
muscles taut, twitching spontaneously.

So innocently meant,
yet so cruelly taken, twisted.
Turned, blades rotating
not believing, not wanting to.
Lies, his judgement.

The sleight of hand, regrets.
To last forever, haunting,
taunting, mocking on repeat.
Apologies spurned,
belief gone, trickled away with all hope.

Heads bowed; body weak.
Broken away, set free.
Her faith shattered,
shards of an exquisite picture
danced away, set free.
Disillusioned, yet free.

Divided by love

Cast asunder
Suddenly crying
Shocked faces
Tears, burnt embers
Cheeks aglow

Chosen, just one
Thrown aside
Like rubbish, lowly
Used, not wanted
Not needed,
Old and tattered

But not
Still new, young
Vibrant
Sadness slivers into the night
Beneath the skin
Writhing, tirelessly
Consuming the soul

Eyes empty
Wandering, lost
Bleakness dawns
No sound
Only a broken heart

Pleasing but lacking
In charm, wit, beauty
No love, all gone
Difficult to connect

The cut of the ribbon
Cathartic, veiled relief
Sailing into the horizon
Distance far deeper
Than words describe

Detached from memory
Aborted by name
Silently she walks
Fate moves in circles

Its powers
Never lie
He will learn
Lessons, many
Drawn into the path
Of those who are weak

Carefree

Shining, it calls to her.
Brighter,
it lights the way.
Enveloping in warm golden haze.
Rape yellowing, a blanket of sunshine
laughing, and dancing carefree,
in the August breeze.

Under the trees
she lay,
watching time.
Sapphire skies, clouds
shapeless, diffusing.
The flaxen sun, penetrating,
glare bouncing off opaqueness.
Protecting those hidden beneath,
yet, observing all.

Swallows plunge, heat reflecting,
their sleek feathers shine.
They speed, low, high,
playful, flying closer.
Notwithstanding, wings rapid
Mesmerising they glide with ease.
Graceful then gone,
new adventures to find.

Death

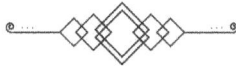

Silently it waits, patiently, plotting its sinister demise.
A collection of souls,
an addiction,
its calling.

It lingers, lengthy, painful
basking in the glory, draining every fragment.
Young or old it has no value
for life.

Stealthily prowling, its victim in sight
abruptly it lunges, the element of surprise.
Shock, then tears
grief follows swiftly,
selfishly it takes.

Emotionless for humanity
soulless and frosted
bereft of sympathy, sentiment or justification.
No immunity.
Ever.

Bound by Love

Frustration,
a crescendo crashing abruptly
only to rise from the depths below,
once more.
Imprisoned, no end in sight, no release.
Merciless they take... trampling minds,
choking life.

Bound by love,
thwarted by resentment.
Ashamed to feel, torn.
Shackled by kin.
Patience escaped,
tolerance hanging like pray in a spider's web.
Bitterness it gnaws,
the inner voice unbearable.

The screams and
turmoil, locked within every thought,
never-ending, never easing
growing diseased.
Changing thoughts from love.
Trapped, the sense of loss,
of what could – should, have been.

Those days, those hours, those minutes...
will never return.
Futile attempts change nothing.
The binds tighten,
no freedom,
enjoyment— a distant memory
of what once was.

Days merge, never ending,
the monotony torturous.
Wings clipped,
an invisible cage,
dark thoughts flit frequently throughout the day.
The beautiful soul,
slowly dying, without notice.
Night brings short relief, peace until dawn.
Bound by love,
shackled by kin.

Never Broken

His face set, determined.
Arms crossed, furrowed brows,
a life of their own.
Cheek scarred,
the outline faint.

Wounds superficial,
words delve deep.
Voices raised, she cowers, startled,
expecting.
The sting, her tears blinked back,
with steely determination.
Eyes wide, challenging.

Flesh hitting flesh, high-pitched,
almost musical.
Anger rising,
her body weakening,
slumped against rain-drenched concrete.
Boots scuffed, dirty, unkempt, mirroring their owner.

His blows reign mightily,
She's helpless to resist.
Surreal numbness, pain follows sharply,
lying limp.
The coldness gives relief...
He walks away, gaze fixed,
humming tunelessly...

It's Raining Again...

The darkness looms once again,
black thunderous clouds
ever-increasing,
as the days pass by.

Will it ever let up?
Will peace descend?
Only so much can be carried
before the legs go weak,
before the body slumps wearily.

The heavens open,
rain pours, drenching skin.
Draining a jaded mind.
The last ounce of strength washed away,
forever.

Is this the last?
Will peace descend?
Nothing more can be carried.
Body and mind surrender... defeated.

A Pauper Shrouded in Gold

Mystical auras,
flitting silently like multi-orb nymphs.
Amethyst cloak in crushed velvet.
Tactile. Hooded.
Envelop weary, wizened shoulders.
Stooped.
Lines etched,
deep within crags of an ash-toned pallor,
fingers gnarled, arthritic and set.

Incense-wafting,
dream catcher glinting.
Destiny spinning, through a glassy spherical
ideology.
Mysteriously communicating
crystal, clear.
Visible only to higher spiritual beings.

Images appear, fleetingly; stories untold.
Disjointed they unfold.
Words spoken— eyes wide in wonderment,
fascination of a world beyond,
predicting the often unimaginable.
A path not yet travelled
craving answers.

Desperate for joy,
for hope.
Security in abundance.
Images appear,
lacking certainty, hope
or clarity.
Messages jumbled,
struggling to piece the future like a patchwork quilt.

Dismissing 'The Towers' turmoil.
Embracing the brightness,
'The Star' shines gaily,
belief is focused on positive words.
Life-worn hands stop spinning
waiting... to see.

Cynics belittle,
believers shirk negativity,
engulfed in spiritual freedom
of their predestined future.
Accepting those invisible shackles
of an unknown journey

Fragility of Life

It hangs, silken, thread-like,
so delicate, a fine balance.
A tightrope of land mines,
waiting.
His focus, a narrowed view,
forging ahead,
oblivious to the perils concealed
within his burgeoning energy fields.

Impeccable to adoring onlookers.
Successful, handsome, ever popular.
Perceived perfection,
at what price?

Inside a colossal emptiness,
pressured by whom?
Himself? Adoring onlookers? Both?
Failure,
an opportunity for improvement.
Failure is failing.
Not an option.

The accolade,
the euphoria,
a euphemism of fake adoration,
each one as insecure as the other.

Magenta-painted talons,
clawing viciously.
Whilst gleaming veneers,
forced into a falsified smile.
Taut, bronzed, perfect— his tattooed skin,
mocking any misdemeanour.

The imaginary jewel-encrusted blade,
twisting mercilessly.
Bloodless pain,
seeping through his wounded core.

The spotlight wanes,
onto another dream-driven hopeful.
Shunned, like an aged dog,
discarded for a new popularity puppy.
Grey storms
siphon any signs of vibrant colour,
like a black and white television, of old.

His life.
Gloomy. Lacking. Desperate.
The emptiness hangs,
he longs to be wanted,
needed; loved by many.

It's gone!
Ain't never coming back.

He only believes there is one choice.
He only believes in one way out.
The fragility of his life hangs, silken thread-like.
He doesn't believe in balance.
He believes there's only one answer.

He believes there's only one decision to make.
He believes it's the right choice.
It's the right time.
The right moment.

He's gone!
Ain't never coming back...

The Lionesses Guardian

Cock-sure,
silvery smattered chest puffed gallantly.
Failure a word not spoken.
He wanted.
He got.
She wanted.
She got.

Patrolling the vast fortress.
Nothing less.
For him.
For her.
The lion.
His lioness.

Mating calls slowly rising,
a distance heard.
With proud stance,
his fierceness,
protecting his coveted pride.
Noble. Majestic.
Staving potential predators away,
from his sweet,
dear innamorato.

Possessively he guards,
His sword invisible.
Valiant
he challenges.

Come forth his cerulean eyes mock.
Wanting, to prove.
Status.
Is everything.

His steel armour, gently moulded,
clothing delicate shoulders.
Oozing warmth from an umbilical connection,
a trembling pulse of devotion,
love, and unspoken words.

Titillating telepathy,
two-minds cemented.
Joined in unison.
Heaving breasts lather
intimate beyond divine expectations.
Bodies and wanton minds,
entwined indefinitely.
Sated.

A forbidden opiate,
absorbed through a porous epidermis.
Laid bare, welcoming.
Her sensual aura,
Hypnotic. Addictive.
Encompassing every inch
of her enchanting feline magnetism.

Powerless.
He follows.

The Invisible Thief

You penetrated me.
Seeping slowly, drowning unsuspecting senses.
A silent thief.
Trespassing into every vulnerable orifice,
suffocating the very essence of life.
Leaving no trail behind, nor any clues.
A first-class invisible thief.

Every cell smothered.
Gasping for breath.
Encasing each victim, squeezing tightly,
the power victorious.
Virtual handcuffs bound,
suffering forevermore.

No warnings.
No translucent glimpse.
No tell-tale bitterness to taste.
No scent of fear.
Just a bitterness of what you claimed.

I breathed you in, lungs filled to capacity.
Odourless, permeating my fragile, venous map.
Toxin-riddled organs,
desperate to survive.
Fighting a battle, one I will never win.

With you,
The invisible thief.

My nerve-filled cortex, besieged first.
Confused. Forgetful. Saturated.
Journey's wiped out,
destinations never quite reached.
Faces void, recognition vanished.
Memories lost forever.

The incessant pounding.
Over and over, a cacophony of drums.
Beating. Loudly.
Scrambling to explode,
those aching, sinewy limbs,
feeble and limp.
Emotions drained.
Once full, now an empty energy tank.

Are you sorrowful?
Regretful?
Do you dwell on such dreadful deeds?
Or do you forge ahead
leaching life from unsuspecting victims?
Silently you prowl. Masterful. Impressive even.
Success reigns on every cellular level.

You kill swiftly, mercilessly.
My suffering your sheer pleasure.
Daily. Slowly. Relentlessly.
Forever lingering.
The pain.
My punishing torment.

I was spared a hurried end.
Why?

The innocent do not know you.
The innocent do not know of your destructive capabilities.
They are blissfully ignorant in their innocence.
As I once were.

You stole my life.
You will steal theirs too.

You. Are.

The Invisible Thief

Continuum

My body has completed its journey,
etched with a myriad of stories.
An empty vessel no longer required
as once was, in youth gone by.

My soul full and satisfied.
Ready for continuum, learning lessons aplenty.
Overflowing with past earthly experiences,
and welcoming
new heavenly challenges.

Don't feel sorrow
I don't
Don't feel sadness
I don't
Don't feel loss
I don't

I smile at those who I've met,
the ones I've cherished and loved.
The ones who caused me sadness,
I can let go and send pure love and peace.
Their life was chosen,
as yours was,
their soul had its own journey,
the destination the same as mine.

My empty shell scattered,
fragments slowly drifting,
carried on the gentle breeze.
Creating new souls, beginning the cycle
of life
I smile, I watch, I see.

You go about your daily tasks,
worrying needlessly.
Always live in the present,
be mindful,
you are truly blessed.
Tomorrow doesn't always follow today...

The countdown is on,
to meet me again.
No one misses their end,
no one is ever late...
The end of your physical embodiment
is only the start of your
souls true journey.

I smile
I watch
I see

Pray friends, smile with me....

Acknowledgement

I started writing poetry back in 2001, a cathartic way of dealing with life's challenges. Whenever the road was rocky, I would cleanse my inner demons with the written word; any unwanted thoughts bubbling up inside me, were excised onto a blank page.

I never intended to publish my writing. My words were raw, emotive and so very personal; never created to share. I believed my thoughts were akin to those in a diary, or a personal journal – for my eyes only.

Yet, deep down, I often considered, that by sharing my thoughts and challenges, maybe - just maybe, it may encourage others to express their feelings too. That slight glimmer of hope, has made the leap from my comfort zone to publishing, worth every uncomfortable second.

Writing has been extremely healing for me, and I really believe anyone can have a creative outlet, whether it's through writing, painting or music; We can all experience positive, physical, and emotional benefits, as I did - and still do.
Try it, you just might like it!

I have to give huge thanks to my publisher, Eloise Attenborough, at Book Bubble Press for not only making me accountable, by setting out a schedule, timeline, and deadlines, but for also giving me the encouragement, self-belief and strength to set my thoughts free. If it hadn't been for Eloise, 'The Invisible Thief' would still be hidden away on my hard drive, never seeing the light of day.

Thank you to my amazing, beautiful children, you make me so proud every day, I love you unconditionally. Without you, life would have no purpose. I hope you follow your dreams, as I am following mine – albeit 46 years late!

My advice to you (for what it's worth!): do what you love, treasure special moments, spend time with loved ones, share your knowledge and help others less fortunate than yourselves. And finally, do what gives you joy and happiness, you won't go far wrong.

Thank you to all my friends and family, (you know who you are!) who have encouraged me all the way. I love you all! I have to say thanks to all those who have purchased my book, I will be eternally grateful, and I hope you enjoy my poetic ramblings, as much as I enjoyed writing them. If you don't enjoy them (and that's okay too!), then maybe pass the book onto someone who might just do – or a drop it off at a local charity shop, I'm a real advocate for recycling.

A special thank you to the unbelievably strong and talented Penny Taylor; a young poet, sadly taken too soon after her long fight with Cystic Fibrosis. She has always been an inspiration to me, and her personal anthology 'The Babble of Bic' has sat proudly on my bookshelf since 1989.

I also want to thank those people, and acknowledge those events, that over the years, have given me the inspiration for my work; without them, this book would never have materialised. We are all on a journey, and as I mature, I have learned to let go of anger, hurt and pain – negative emotions serve no purpose, they are futile and hold us back from following our dreams.

'Strength is within us; we need to believe in its ability, to guide us through those difficult times'.

Angelica. x

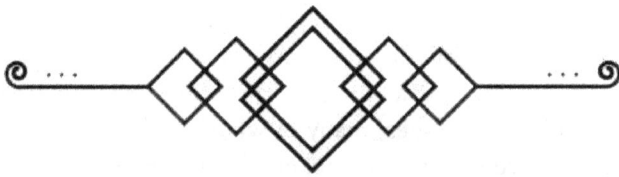

About the author

Always a lover of words, but never dreamed her life could ever encompass her long-lived passion. A born creative; Angelica has forged a successful career, over the last decade as an award-winning horse photographer, with commissions both in the UK and internationally. Angelica lives in Cheshire, England with her two children, and three dogs. A passionate animal lover, she has ridden horses from a young age and has owned several horses.

Angelica has enjoyed a diverse work life, from teaching fitness classes to owning a construction company, variety always the spice of Angelica's eclectic life. Being a free-spirited Aquarian, she has always preferred the flexible world of self-employment and has relished the challenges of wide-ranging adventures.

After a near-death experience, between 2003-2006, Angelica suffered a serious brain injury, caused by carbon monoxide poisoning. Unable to read for over three years she suffered a multitude of health issues, many of which are on going.

Angelica is a true fighter and acknowledges the CO incident changed her life irrevocably; writing has helped her through some of the most challenging times of her life. She now is an ambassador and director of www.co-gassafety.co.uk, a charity, which raises awareness of carbon monoxide poisoning and its dangers.

Angelica has appeared on TV, radio, print and online media with her incredible story and charity work. She is also an inspirational speaker and business coach.

www.angelicaryderwood.com
email angelica@angelicaryderwood.com
fb: angelicaryderwood
Insta: @angelicaryderwood
Twitter: @AngelicaRyderW1

www.ingramcontent.com/pod-product-compliance
Lightning Source LLC
Chambersburg PA
CBHW071905020426
42331CB00010B/2685